THIS WALKER BOOK BELONGS TO:

_____

_____

_____

_____

# · Michael Foreman's · NURSERY RHYMES

# ❖ Michael Foreman's ❖
# Nursery Rhymes

Foreword by Iona Opie

WALKER BOOKS
AND SUBSIDIARIES
LONDON ❖ BOSTON ❖ SYDNEY

First published 1991 by Walker Books Ltd
87 Vauxhall Walk, London SE11 5HJ

This edition published 2003

2 4 6 8 10 9 7 5 3 1

Illustrations © 1991, 1998 Michael Foreman
Foreward © 1991 Iona Opie

This book has been typeset in Garamond

Printed in China

British Library Cataloguing in Publication Data:
a catalogue record for this book is available from the British Library

ISBN: 0-7445-9820-6

*For our boys Ben and Jack, and Sam and Chloe*

# FOREWORD

As the poet John Clare said in 1825, nursery rhymes "live on as common to memory as the seasons, and as familiar to children even as the rain and spring flowers." They are the first furnishings of the mind; the bottom-most layer of the comfortable hereditary clutter of mottoes, proverbs and half-remembered tales that we use to ornament conversations throughout our lives, knowing that they are common currency.

Everyone is familiar with the efficacy of Little Jack Horner's thumb, the sad state of Mother Hubbard's cupboard, and the inadequate reason for the quarrel between Tweedledum and Tweedledee, so that a passing reference in an MP's speech will save much tedious explanation. Wherever the English tongue is spoken, the *lingua franca* of nursery rhymes has been used to tell jokes and sell merchandise. Poets, too, have borrowed the old magic of phrases like "Over the hills and far away" to launch themselves on fresh odysseys.

To a child, nursery rhymes are full of satisfactions: other people's misdemeanours (*Little Boy Blue*) and disasters (*Dr Foster*); romances (*Lilies are white, rosemary's green*); amazements (*Robin the Bobbin*) and mysteries (*Ladybird, Ladybird*); irrefutable logic (*Jumping Joan*); and happy accompaniments to the first steps in learning (*A was an Apple Pie; One, two, buckle my shoe*). Their charm lies in their poeticality, and in the effortless absurdity with which porridge and pipes and pussy cats appear in improbable contexts, and the moon sails scarcely higher than a house-top. Those who enjoy language as a toy and entertainment in itself, will find that the words of nursery rhymes seem intoxicated by their own nonsense and, as at the cocktail party in Gormenghast, are *playing on their own*.

To an adult, the rhymes are, above all, serviceable. Some can lull or excite the smallest infant, according to requirement; others can transfix a two-year-old in mid-rampage, as well as distract him when, inevitably, he comes to grief. On dismal grey afternoons a nursery rhyme book can hold spell-bound a whole houseful of malcontents – especially if, like this book, it is illustrated by an artist who possesses his own spy-glass and can see into the far corners of the old nursery dramas, finding possibilities and consequences never imagined before.

The nursery rhyme repertoire stays remarkably constant. What need for new nursery rhymes when there are always new children? To the delight of nursery rhymes, however, there is no end. Here they are, for our enjoyment: as much for the four-year-old bumpetting up and down on the sofa to a chant of "Charley, Charley, stole the barley" as (let it be confessed) for the grandmother who croaks "Lavender's blue" to herself as she takes a hot bath. We can truly say with Robert Graves,

> …may the gift of heavenly peace
>     And glory for all time
> Keep the boy Tom who tending geese
>     First made the nursery rhyme.

*Iona Opie*

## GOOSE FEATHERS

Cackle, cackle, Mother Goose,
Have you any feathers loose?
Truly have I, pretty fellow,
Half enough to fill a pillow.
Here are quills, take one or two,
And down to make a bed for you.

## HUSH-A-BYE, BABY

Hush-a-bye, baby,
  On the tree top,
When the wind blows,
  The cradle will rock;
When the bough breaks
  The cradle will fall,
Down tumbles baby,
  Cradle and all.

## ROCK-A-BYE, BABY

Rock-a-bye, baby,
  Thy cradle is green,
Father's a nobleman,
  Mother's a queen;
And Betty's a lady,
  And wears a gold ring;
And Johnny's a drummer,
  And drums for the king.

## HUSH, LITTLE BABY

Hush, little baby, don't say a word,
Daddy's going to buy you a mocking bird;
If that mocking bird don't sing,
Daddy's going to buy you a diamond ring;
If that diamond ring turns to brass,
Daddy's going to buy you a looking glass;
If that looking glass gets broke,
Daddy's going to buy you a billy goat;
If that billy goat runs away–
Daddy'll buy you another, today.

## BYE, BABY BUNTING

Bye, baby bunting,
Daddy's gone a-hunting,
Gone to get a rabbit skin
To wrap the baby bunting in.

## SLEEP, BABY, SLEEP

Sleep, baby, sleep,
Our cottage vale is deep;
A little lamb is on the green,
With woolly fleece
    so soft and clean–
Sleep, baby, sleep.

13

## ROUND AND ROUND THE GARDEN

Round and round the garden
Like a teddy bear;
One step, two step,
Tickle you under there!

## THIS LITTLE PIG

This little pig went to market,
This little pig stayed at home,
This little pig had roast beef,
This little pig had none,
And this little pig cried, Wee-wee-wee,
 All the way home.

## THIS IS THE WAY THE LADIES RIDE

This is the way the ladies ride:
Tri, tre, tre, tree,
Tri, tre, tre, tree!
This is the way the ladies ride:
Tri, tre, tre, tre, tri-tre-tre-tree!

This is the way the gentlemen ride:
Gallop-a-trot,
Gallop-a-trot!
This is the way the gentlemen ride:
Gallop-a-gallop-a-trot!

## RIDE A COCK-HORSE

Ride a cock-horse to Banbury Cross,
To see a fine lady upon a white horse;
Rings on her fingers and bells on her toes,
And she shall have music wherever she goes.

## TO MARKET, TO MARKET

To market, to market, to buy a fat pig,
  Home again, home again, jiggety-jig;
To market, to market, to buy a fat hog,
  Home again, home again, jiggety-jog.

## A FARMER WENT TROTTING

A farmer went trotting
Upon his grey mare,
  Bumpety, bumpety, bump!
With his daughter behind him
So rosy and fair,
  Lumpety, lumpety, lump!

A raven cried, Croak!
And they all tumbled down,
  Bumpety, bumpety, bump!
The mare broke her knees
And the farmer his crown,
  Lumpety, lumpety, lump!

This mischievous raven
Flew laughing away,
  Bumpety, bumpety, bump!
And vowed he would serve them
The same the next day,
  Lumpety, lumpety, lump!

## ROW THE BOAT

Row, row, row the boat
Gently down the stream,
Merrily, merrily, merrily, merrily,
Life is but a dream.

## SEE-SAW

See-saw, Margery Daw,
Jacky shall have a new master;
Jacky shall have but a penny a day,
Because he can't work any faster.

## DANCE TO YOUR DADDY

Dance to your daddy,
  My little babby,
Dance to your daddy,
  My little lamb!
You shall have a fishy
  In a little dishy,
You shall have a fishy
  When the boat comes in.

## LITTLE BOY BLUE

Little Boy Blue,
  Come blow your horn,
The sheep's in the meadow,
  The cow's in the corn;
But where is the boy
  Who looks after the sheep?
He's under a haycock,
  Fast asleep.
Will you wake him?
  No, not I,
For if I do,
  He's sure to cry.

## BAA, BAA, BLACK SHEEP

Baa, baa, black sheep,
  Have you any wool?
Yes sir, yes sir,
  Three bags full:
One for the master,
  And one for the dame,
And one for the little boy
  Who lives down the lane.

## LITTLE BO-PEEP

Little Bo-peep has lost her sheep,
  And doesn't know where to find them.
Leave them alone, and they'll come home,
  Bringing their tails behind them.

Little Bo-peep fell fast asleep,
  And dreamt she heard them bleating.
But when she awoke, she found it a joke,
  For they were still a-fleeting.

Then up she took her little crook,
  Determined for to find them.
She found them indeed, but it made her heart bleed,
  For they'd left their tails behind them.

It happened one day, as Bo-peep did stray
  Into a meadow hard by,
There she espied their tails side by side,
  All hung on a tree to dry.

She heaved a sigh and wiped her eye,
  And over the hillocks went rambling,
And tried what she could, as a shepherdess should,
  To tack again each to its lambkin.

## MARY HAD A LITTLE LAMB

Mary had a little lamb,
  Its fleece was white as snow;
And everywhere that Mary went
  The lamb was sure to go.

It followed her to school one day,
  That was against the rule;
It made the children laugh and play,
  To see a lamb in school.

And so the teacher turned it out,
  But still it lingered near,
And waited patiently about
  Till Mary did appear.

Why does the lamb love Mary so?
  The eager children cry;
Why, Mary loves the lamb, you know,
  The teacher did reply.

## MARY, MARY

Mary, Mary, quite contrary,
How does your garden grow?
With silver bells and cockle shells,
And pretty maids all in a row.

## LITTLE MISS MUFFET

Little Miss Muffet
Sat on a tuffet,
Eating her curds and whey;
There came a big spider,
Who sat down beside her
And frightened Miss Muffet away.

## PUSSY CAT

Pussy cat, pussy cat,
  Where have you been?
I've been to London
  To look at the queen.
Pussy cat, pussy cat,
  What did you there?
I frightened a little mouse
  Under her chair.

## PRETTY MAID

Pretty maid, pretty maid,
Where have you been?
Gathering roses
To give to the queen.
Pretty maid, pretty maid,
What gave she you?
She gave me a diamond,
As big as my shoe.

23

## HUMPTY DUMPTY

Humpty Dumpty sat on a wall,
Humpty Dumpty had a great fall.
All the king's horses and all the king's men,
Couldn't put Humpty together again.

## THE GRAND OLD DUKE OF YORK

Oh, the grand old Duke of York,
  He had ten thousand men;
He marched them up to the top of the hill,
  And he marched them down again.
And when they were up, they were up,
  And when they were down, they were down,
And when they were only half-way up,
  They were neither up nor down.

### UNDER A HILL

There was an old woman
  Lived under a hill,
And if she's not gone
  She lives there still.

## JACK AND JILL

Jack and Jill
Went up the hill,
To fetch a pail of water;
Jack fell down,
And broke his crown,
And Jill came tumbling after.

Then up Jack got,
And home did trot,
As fast as he could caper,
To old Dame Dob,
Who patched his nob,
With vinegar and brown paper.

When Jill came in,
How she did grin,
To see Jack's paper plaster;
Her mother, vexed,
Did whip her next,
For laughing at Jack's disaster.

Now Jack did laugh,
And Jill did cry,
But her tears did soon abate;
Then Jill did say,
That they should play
At see-saw across the gate.

## TWINKLE, TWINKLE, LITTLE STAR

Twinkle, twinkle, little star,
How I wonder what you are!
Up above the world so high,
Like a diamond in the sky.

## HICKORY, DICKORY, DOCK

Hickory, dickory, dock,
The mouse ran up the clock.
  The clock struck one,
  The mouse ran down,
Hickory, dickory, dock.

## JACK BE NIMBLE

Jack be nimble,
Jack be quick,
Jack jump over
The candlestick.

## WEE WILLIE WINKIE

Wee Willie Winkie runs through the town,
Upstairs and downstairs in his nightgown,
Rapping at the window, crying through the lock,
Are the children all in bed, for now it's eight o'clock?

## HEY DIDDLE DIDDLE

Hey diddle diddle,
The cat and the fiddle,
The cow jumped over the moon;
The little dog laughed
To see such sport,
And the dish ran away with the spoon.

## PUSSY CAT MOLE

Pussy cat Mole jumped over a coal
And in her best petticoat burnt a great hole.
Poor pussy's weeping, she'll have no more milk
Until her best petticoat's mended with silk.

## PUSS UP THE PLUM TREE

Diddlety, diddlety, dumpty,
The cat ran up the plum tree;
Half a crown to fetch her down,
Diddlety, diddlety, dumpty.

## THREE LITTLE KITTENS

Three little kittens
They lost their mittens,
  And they began to cry,
Oh, mother dear,
We sadly fear
  That we have lost our mittens.
What! lost your mittens,
You naughty kittens!
  Then you shall have no pie.
  Mee-ow, mee-ow, mee-ow.
  No, you shall have no pie.

The three little kittens
They found their mittens,
  And they began to cry,
Oh, mother dear,
See here, see here,
  For we have found our mittens.
Put on your mittens,
You silly kittens,
  And you shall have some pie.
  Purr-r, purr-r, purr-r,
  Oh, let us have some pie.

The three little kittens
Put on their mittens,
  And soon ate up the pie;
Oh, mother dear,
We greatly fear
  That we have soiled our mittens.
What! soiled your mittens,
You naughty kittens!
  Then they began to sigh,
  Mee-ow, mee-ow, mee-ow,
  Then they began to sigh.

The three little kittens
They washed their mittens,
  And hung them out to dry;
Oh! mother dear,
Do you not hear,
  That we have washed our mittens.
What! washed your mittens,
Then you're good kittens,
  But I smell a rat close by.
  Mee-ow, mee-ow, mee-ow,
  We smell a rat close by.

## DING, DONG, BELL

Ding, dong, bell,
Pussy's in the well.
Who put her in?
Little Johnny Green.
Who pulled her out?
Little Tommy Stout.
What a naughty boy was that,
To try to drown poor pussy cat,
Who never did him any harm,
And killed the mice in his father's barn.

## I LOVE LITTLE PUSSY

I love little pussy,
　Her coat is so warm,
And if I don't hurt her
　She'll do me no harm.
So I'll not pull her tail,
　Nor drive her away,
But pussy and I
　Very gently will play.
She shall sit by my side,
　And I'll give her some food;
And pussy will love me
　Because I am good.

## SIX LITTLE MICE

Six little mice sat down to spin;
Pussy passed by and she peeped in.
What are you doing, my little men?
Weaving coats for gentlemen.
Shall I come in and cut off your threads?
No, no Mistress Pussy, you'd bite off our heads.
Oh, no, I'll not; I'll help you to spin.
That may be so, but you can't come in.

## PUSSY CAT, PUSSY CAT

Pussy cat, pussy cat,
  wilt thou be mine,
Thou shalt neither wash dishes
  nor feed the swine:
But sit on a cushion
  and sew a silk seam,
And eat fine strawberries,
  sugar and cream.

### WHO'S THAT RINGING?

Who's that ringing at my door bell?
  A little pussy cat that isn't very well.
Rub its little nose with a little mutton fat,
  That's the best cure for a little pussy cat.

### PUSSICAT, WUSSICAT

Pussicat, wussicat, with a white foot,
When is your wedding, and I'll come to it.
The beer's to brew, the bread's to bake,
Pussicat, wussicat, don't be too late.

## SING, SING

Sing, sing,
  What shall I sing?
The cat's run away
  With the pudding string!
Do, do,
  What shall I do?
The cat's run away
  With the pudding too!

## PUSS CAME DANCING

Puss came dancing out of a barn
With a pair of bagpipes under her arm;
She could sing nothing but, Fiddle cum fee,
The mouse has married the humble-bee.
Pipe, cat–dance, mouse–
We'll have a wedding at our good house.

## AS I WAS GOING TO ST IVES

As I was going to St Ives,
I met a man with seven wives;
Each wife had seven sacks,
Each sack had seven cats,
Each cat had seven kits;
Kits, cats, sacks and wives,
How many were going to St Ives?

## BONNY BOBBY SHAFTO

Bobby Shafto's gone to sea,
Silver buckles at his knee;
He'll come back and marry me,
Bonny Bobby Shafto!

Bobby Shafto's tall and fair
Combing down his yellow hair;
He's my love for ever more;
Bonny Bobby Shafto.

## I Saw A Ship

I saw a ship a-sailing,
  A-sailing on the sea,
And oh but it was laden,
  With pretty things for thee.

There were comfits
  in the cabin,
  And apples in the hold;
The sails were made
  of silk,
  And the masts were
    all of gold.

The four-and-twenty sailors,
  That stood between the decks,
Were four-and-twenty white mice
  With chains about their necks.

The captain was a duck
  With a packet on his back,
And when the ship began to move,
  The captain said, Quack! Quack!

42

### LITTLE TEE-WEE

Little Tee-wee,
He went to sea,
In an open boat;
And when it was afloat,
The little boat bended.
My story's ended.

### THREE WISE MEN

Three wise men of Gotham
Went to sea in a bowl;
If the bowl had been stronger,
My story would have been longer.

### ROBINSON CRUSOE

Poor old Robinson Crusoe!
Poor old Robinson Crusoe!
He made him a coat,
Of an old nanny goat,
What a clever fellow to do so!
With a ring a ting tang,
And a ring a ting tang,
Poor old Robinson Crusoe!

## IF ALL THE SEAS

If all the seas were one sea,
What a *great* sea that would be!
If all the trees were one tree,
What a *great* tree that would be!
And if all the axes were one axe,
What a *great* axe that would be!
And if all the men were one man,
What a *great* man that would be!
And if the *great* man took the *great* axe,
And cut down the *great* tree,
And let it fall into the *great* sea,
What a splish-splash that would be!

## FEE, FI, FO, FUM

Fee, fi, fo, fum,
I smell the blood of an Englishman;
Be he alive or be he dead,
I'll grind his bones to make my bread.

## I'M THE KING OF THE CASTLE

I'm the king of the castle,
Get down you dirty rascal.

45

## ELSIE MARLEY

Elsie Marley is grown so fine,
She won't get up to feed the swine,
But lies in bed till eight or nine.
   Lazy Elsie Marley.

## HECTOR PROTECTOR

Hector Protector was dressed all in green;
Hector Protector was sent to the queen.
The queen did not like him,
No more did the king;
So Hector Protector was sent back again.

## SING A SONG OF SIXPENCE

Sing a song of sixpence,
  A pocket full of rye;
Four-and-twenty blackbirds,
  Baked in a pie.

When the pie was opened,
  The birds began to sing;
Wasn't that a dainty dish,
  To set before the king?

The king was in his counting-house,
  Counting out his money;
The queen was in the parlour,
  Eating bread and honey.

The maid was in the garden,
  Hanging out the clothes,
There came a great big blackbird,
  And nipped off her nose.

## OLD KING COLE

Old King Cole
Was a merry old soul,
And a merry old soul was he;
He called for his pipe,
And he called for his bowl,
And he called for his fiddlers three.

Every fiddler, he had a fiddle,
And a very fine fiddle had he;
Twee tweedle dee, tweedle dee, went the fiddlers.
Oh, there's none so rare,
As can compare
With King Cole and his fiddlers three!

## THE QUEEN OF HEARTS

The Queen of Hearts
She made some tarts,
All on a summer's day;
The Knave of Hearts
He stole the tarts,
And took them clean away.

The King of Hearts
Called for the tarts,
And beat the knave full sore;
The Knave of Hearts
Brought back the tarts,
And vowed he'd steal no more.

## TO THE MAGPIE

Magpie, magpie, flutter and flee,
Turn up your tail and good luck come to me.

## TWO LITTLE DICKY BIRDS

Two little dicky birds sitting on a wall,
One named Peter, one named Paul.
Fly away Peter! Fly away Paul!
Come back Peter! Come back Paul!

## LITTLE ROBIN REDBREAST

Little Robin Redbreast
Sat upon a rail;
Niddle noddle went his head,
Wiggle waggle went his tail.

## LITTLE ROBIN REDBREAST

Little Robin Redbreast sat upon a tree,
Up went pussy cat, and down went he;
Down came pussy, and away Robin ran;
Says little Robin Redbreast, Catch me if you can.
Little Robin Redbreast jumped upon a wall,
Pussy cat jumped after him, and almost got a fall;
Little Robin chirped and sang, and what did pussy say?
Pussy cat said, Mew, and Robin jumped away.

## COCK ROBIN'S COURTSHIP

Cock Robin got up early
  At the break of day,
And went to Jenny's window
  To sing a roundelay.
He sang Cock Robin's love
  To little Jenny Wren,
And when he got unto the end
  Then he began again.

# THE DEATH AND BURIAL OF COCK ROBIN

Who killed Cock Robin?
  I, said the sparrow,
  With my bow and arrow,
I killed Cock Robin.

Who saw him die?
  I, said the fly,
  With my little eye,
I saw him die.

Who caught his blood?
  I said the fish,
  With my little dish,
I caught his blood.

Who'll make his shroud?
  I, said the beetle,
  With my thread and needle,
I'll make the shroud.

Who'll dig his grave?
  I, said the owl,
  With my pick and shovel,
I'll dig his grave.

Who'll be the parson?
  I, said the rook,
  With my little book,
I'll be the parson.

Who'll be the clerk?
  I, said the lark,
  If it's not in the dark,
I'll be the clerk.

Who'll carry the link?
  I, said the linnet,
  I'll fetch it in a minute,
I'll carry the link.

Who'll be chief mourner?
  I, said the dove,
  I mourn for my love,
I'll be chief mourner.

Who'll carry the coffin?
  I, said the kite,
  If it's not through the night,
I'll carry the coffin.

Who'll bear the pall?
  We, said the wren,
  Both the cock and the hen,
We'll bear the pall.

Who'll sing a psalm?
  I, said the thrush,
  As she sat on a bush,
I'll sing a psalm.

Who'll toll the bell?
  I, said the bull,
  Because I can pull,
I'll toll the bell.

All the birds of the air
  Fell a-sighing and a-sobbing,
When they heard the bell toll
  For poor Cock Robin.

## LITTLE BIRD

Once I saw a little bird
  Come hop, hop, hop;
So I cried, Little bird,
  Will you stop, stop, stop?

I was going to the window
  To say, How do you do?
But he shook his little tail,
  And far away he flew.

## THE CUCKOO

The cuckoo is a merry bird,
She sings as she flies;
She brings us good tidings,
And tells us no lies.

She sucks little birds' eggs
To make her voice clear,
That she may sing Cuckoo!
Three months in the year.

## CUCKOO, CUCKOO

Cuckoo, cuckoo,
What do you do?
In April
I open my bill;
In May
I sing night and day;
In June
I change my tune;
In July
Away I fly;
In August
Away I must.

## CHOOK, CHOOK

Chook, chook, chook, chook, chook,
  Good morning, Mrs Hen.
How many chickens have you got?
  Madam, I've got ten.
Four of them are yellow,
  And four of them are brown,
And two of them are speckled red,
  The nicest in the town.

## HIGGLETY, PIGGLETY, POP!

Higglety, pigglety, pop!
The dog has eaten the mop;
  The pig's in a hurry,
  The cat's in a flurry,
Higglety, pigglety, pop!

## GRANDFA' GRIG

Grandfa' Grig
Had a pig,
In a field of clover;
Piggy died,
Grandfa' cried,
And all the fun was over.

## LITTLE PUSS

As Pussy sat upon the step
Taking the nice fresh air,
A neighbour's little dog came by,
Ah, Pussy, are you there?
Good morning, Mistress Pussy Cat,
Come, tell me how you do?
Quite well, I thank you, Puss replied;
Now tell me how are you?

## IF I HAD A DONKEY

If I had a donkey that wouldn't go,
Would I beat him? Oh no, no.
I'd put him in the barn and give him some corn,
The best little donkey that ever was born.

## BOW-WOW

Bow-wow, says the dog,
Mew, mew, says the cat,
Grunt, grunt, goes the hog,
And squeak, goes the rat;
Tu-whu, says the owl,
Caw, caw, says the crow,
Quack, quack, says the duck,
And what cuckoos say you know.

## MY LITTLE DOG

Oh where, oh where has my little dog gone?
  Oh where, oh where can he be?
With his ears cut short and his tail cut long,
  Oh where, oh where is he?

## THREE BLIND MICE

Three blind mice! Three blind mice!
See how they run! See how they run!
They all ran after the farmer's wife,
Who cut off their tails with a carving knife,
Did you ever see such a thing in your life,
　　　　As three blind mice?

## HICKETY, PICKETY

Hickety, pickety, my black hen,
She lays eggs for gentlemen;
Gentlemen come every day
To see what my black hen doth lay,
Sometimes nine and sometimes ten,
Hickety, pickety, my black hen.

## ONE, TWO, THREE, FOUR, FIVE

One, two, three, four, five,
Once I caught a fish alive,
Six, seven, eight, nine, ten,
Then I let it go again.

## IF WISHES WERE HORSES

If wishes were horses
Beggars would ride;
If turnips were watches
I would wear one by my side.

## LITTLE FISHES

Little fishes in a brook,
Father caught them on a hook,
Mother fried them in a pan,
Johnnie eats them like a man.

## HARK, HARK

Hark, hark,
The dogs do bark,
The beggars are coming to town;
Some in rags,
And some in jags,
And one in a velvet gown.

## THE NORTH WIND

The north wind doth blow,
And we shall have snow,
And what will poor Robin do then?
 Poor thing.
He'll sit in a barn,
And keep himself warm,
And hide his head under his wing,
 Poor thing.

## CHRISTMAS IS COMING

Christmas is coming,
  The geese are getting fat,
Please to put a penny
  In an old man's hat;
If you haven't a penny,
  A ha'penny will do,
If you haven't got a ha'penny,
  God bless you!

## JINGLE BELLS

Jingle, bells! Jingle, bells!
  Jingle all the way.
Oh, what fun it is to ride
  In a one-horse open sleigh.

## CHRISTMAS

Christmas comes but once a year
And when it comes it brings good cheer,
A pocketful of money, and a cellar full of beer,
And a good fat pig to last you all the year.

## THE TWELVE DAYS OF CHRISTMAS

On the first day of Christmas,
My true love sent to me
A partridge in a pear tree.

The second day of Christmas,
My true love sent to me
Two turtle doves, and
A partridge in a pear tree.

The third day of Christmas,
My true love sent to me
Three French hens,
Two turtle doves, and
A partridge in a pear tree.

The fourth day of Christmas,
My true love sent to me
Four colly birds,
Three French hens,
Two turtle doves, and
A partridge in a pear tree.

65

The fifth day of Christmas,
My true love sent to me
Five gold rings,
Four colly birds,
Three French hens,
Two turtle doves, and
A partridge in a pear tree.

The sixth day of Christmas,
My true love sent to me
Six geese a-laying,
Five gold rings,
Four colly birds,
Three French hens,
Two turtle doves, and
A partridge in a pear tree.

The seventh day of Christmas,
My true love sent to me
Seven swans a-swimming,
Six geese a-laying,
Five gold rings,
Four colly birds,
Three French hens,
Two turtle doves, and
A partridge in a pear tree.

The eighth day of Christmas,
My true love sent to me
Eight maids a-milking,
Seven swans a-swimming,
Six geese a-laying,
Five gold rings,
Four colly birds,
Three French hens,
Two turtle doves, and
A partridge in a pear tree.

The ninth day of Christmas,
My true love sent to me
Nine drummers drumming,
Eight maids a-milking,
Seven swans a-swimming,
Six geese a-laying,
Five gold rings,
Four colly birds,
Three French hens,
Two turtle doves, and
A partridge in a pear tree.

The tenth day of Christmas,
My true love sent to me
Ten pipers piping,
Nine drummers drumming,
Eight maids a-milking,
Seven swans a-swimming,
Six geese a-laying,
Five gold rings,
Four colly birds,
Three French hens,
Two turtle doves, and
A partridge in a pear tree.

The eleventh day of Christmas,
My true love sent to me
Eleven ladies dancing,
Ten pipers piping,
Nine drummers drumming,
Eight maids a-milking,
Seven swans a-swimming,
Six geese a-laying,
Five gold rings,
Four colly birds,
Three French hens,
Two turtle doves, and
A partridge in a pear tree.

The twelfth day of Christmas,
My true love sent to me
Twelve lords a-leaping,
Eleven ladies dancing,
Ten pipers piping,
Nine drummers drumming,
Eight maids a-milking,
Seven swans a-swimming,
Six geese a-laying,
Five gold rings,
Four colly birds,
Three French hens,
Two turtle doves, and
A partridge in a pear tree.

## GOD BLESS THE MASTER

God bless the master of this house,
The mistress bless also,
And all the little children
That round the table go;
And all your kin and kinsmen,
That dwell both far and near,
I wish you a merry Christmas,
And a happy New Year.

## MARCH WINDS

March winds and April showers
Bring forth May flowers.

## GOOD MORNING

Good morning, Mistress and Master,
I wish you a happy day;
Please to smell my garland
'Cause it is the first of May.

A branch of May I have brought you,
And at your door I stand;
It is but a sprout, but it's well budded out,
The work of our Lord's hand.

## THE FIRST DAY OF MAY

The fair maid who, the first of May,
Goes to the fields at break of day,
And washes in dew from the hawthorn tree,
Will ever after handsome be.

## THE BOUGHS DO SHAKE

The boughs do shake and the bells do ring,
So merrily comes our harvest in,
Our harvest in, our harvest in,
So merrily comes our harvest in.

We've ploughed, we've sowed,
We've reaped, we've mowed,
We've got our harvest in.

## THE APPLE PIP

Once I found an apple pip
And stuck it in the ground,
When I came to look at it
A tiny shoot I found.

The shoot grew up and up each day;
It soon became a tree.
I picked the rosy apples then
And ate them for my tea.

## RIPE APPLES

Here is the tree with leaves so green,
Here are ripe apples that hang between,
When the wind blows,
The apples do fall
Into a basket which gathers them all.

## MY LITTLE NUT TREE

I had a little nut tree,
  Nothing would it bear
But a silver nutmeg
  And a golden pear;
The King of Spain's daughter
  Came to visit me,
And all for the sake
  Of my little nut tree.

### DAISIES

Daisies are our silver,
Buttercups our gold;
I'd not exchange these glowing flowers
For heaps of wealth untold.

### ROSES

Roses are red,
  Violets are blue,
Sugar is sweet
  And so are you.

### LILIES

Lilies are white,
  Rosemary's green,
When I am king,
  You shall be queen.

## LAVENDER'S BLUE, DILLY DILLY

Lavender's blue, dilly dilly, lavender's green,
When I am king, dilly dilly, you shall be queen;
Call up your men, dilly dilly, set them to work,
Some to the plough, dilly dilly, some to the cart;
Some to make hay, dilly dilly, some to thresh corn,
While you and I, dilly dilly, keep ourselves warm.

## HE LOVES ME

He loves me.
  He don't!
He'll have me.
  He won't!
He would
  if he could.
But he can't.
  So he don't.

## CURLY LOCKS

Curly locks, curly locks,
  Wilt thou be mine?
Thou shalt not wash dishes
  Nor yet feed the swine,
But sit on a cushion
  And sew a fine seam,
And feed upon strawberries,
  Sugar and cream.

## THE MILLER

O the little rusty dusty miller,
Dusty was his coat,
Dusty was his colour,
Dusty was the kiss
I got from the miller;
If I had my pockets
Full of gold and siller,
I would give it all
To my dusty miller.

## A LITTLE HUSBAND

I had a little husband,
No bigger than my thumb;
I put him in a pint-pot
And there I bid him drum.
I bought a little horse
That galloped up and down;
I bridled him, and saddled him
And sent him out of town.
I gave him a pair of garters
To garter up his hose,
And a little silk handkerchief,
To wipe his snotty nose.

## A LITTLE GIRL

When I was a little girl,
  About seven years old,
I hadn't got a petticoat,
  To keep me from the cold.

So I went into Darlington,
  That pretty little town,
And there I bought a petticoat,
  A cloak and a gown.

I went into the woods,
  And built me a kirk,
And all the birds of the air,
  They helped me to work.

The hawk, with his long claws,
  Pulled down the stone,
The dove, with her rough bill,
  Brought me them home.

The parrot was the clergyman,
  The peacock was the clerk,
The bullfinch played the organ,
  And we made merry work.

## LITTLE LAD

Little lad, little lad,
  Where were you born?
Far off in Lancashire,
  Under a thorn,
Where they sup butter-milk
  With a ram's horn;
And a pumpkin scoop'd
  With a yellow rim,
Is the bonny bowl
  They breakfast in.

## LITTLE BLUE BEN

Little Blue Ben, who lives in the glen,
Keeps a blue cat and one blue hen,
Which lays of blue eggs a score and ten;
Where shall I find the little Blue Ben?

## A LITTLE BOY

When I was a little boy
My mammy kept me in,
Now I am a great boy
I'm fit to serve the king;
I can hand a musket,
And I can smoke a pipe,
And I can kiss a bonny girl
At twelve o'clock at night.

## GEORGIE PORGIE

Georgie Porgie, pudding and pie,
Kissed the girls and made them cry;
When the boys came out to play,
Georgie Porgie ran away.

## ONE, TWO

One, two,
Buckle my shoe;
Three, four,
Knock at the door;
Five, six,
Pick up sticks;
Seven, eight,
Lay them straight;
Nine, ten,
A big fat hen;
Eleven, twelve,
Dig and delve;
Thirteen, fourteen,
Maids a-courting;
Fifteen, sixteen,
Maids in the kitchen;
Seventeen, eighteen,
Maids in waiting;
Nineteen, twenty,
My plate's empty.

## I CAN

I can tie my shoe lace
I can comb my hair
I can wash my hands and face
And dry myself with care.

I can brush my teeth, too,
And button up my frocks;
I can say, How do you do?
And put on both my socks.

## A WAS AN APPLE PIE

A was an apple pie,
B bit it,
C cut it,
D dealt it,
E eat it,
F fought for it,
G got it,
H had it,
I inspected it,
J jumped for it,
K kept it,
L longed for it,
M mourned for it,
N nodded at it,
O opened it,
P peeped in it,
Q quartered it,
R ran for it,
S stole it,
T took it,
U upset it,
V viewed it,
W wanted it,
X, Y, Z, and ampersand
All wished for a piece in hand.

## SIMPLE SIMON

Simple Simon met a pieman,
  Going to the fair;
Says Simple Simon to the pieman,
  Let me taste your ware.

Says the pieman to Simple Simon,
  Show me first your penny;
Says Simple Simon to the pieman,
  Indeed I have not any.

Simple Simon went a-fishing,
  For to catch a whale;
All the water he had got
  Was in his mother's pail.

Simple Simon went to look
  If plums grew on a thistle;
He pricked his finger very much,
  Which made poor Simon whistle.

He went for water in a sieve,
  But soon it all ran through;
And now poor Simple Simon
  Bids you all adieu.

## TOM, THE PIPER'S SON

Tom, he was a piper's son,
He learnt to play when he was young,
But all the tunes that he could play
Was, "Over the hills and far away".
    Over the hills and a great way off,
    The wind shall blow my top-knot off.

Tom with his pipe made such a noise,
That he pleased both the girls and boys;
They all danced while he did play,
"Over the hills and far away".
    Over the hills and a great way off,
    The wind shall blow my top-knot off.

Tom with his pipe did play with such skill
That those who heard him could never keep still,
As soon as he played they began for to dance,
Even pigs on their hind legs would after him prance.
Over the hills and a great way off,
The wind shall blow my top-knot off.

As Dolly was milking her cow one day,
Tom took his pipe and began for to play;
So Doll and the cow danced "The Cheshire Round",
Till the pail was broken and the milk ran on the ground.
Over the hills and a great way off,
The wind shall blow my top-knot off.

He met old Dame Trot with a basket of eggs,
He used his pipe and she used her legs;
She danced about till the eggs were all broke,
She began for to fret, but he laughed at the joke.
Over the hills and a great way off,
The wind shall blow my top-knot off.

Tom saw a cross fellow was beating an ass,
Heavy laden with pots, pans, dishes and glass;
He took out his pipe and he played them a tune,
And the poor donkey's load was lightened full soon.
Over the hills and a great way off,
The wind shall blow my top-knot off.

### THERE WAS AN OLD WOMAN

There was an old woman tossed up in a blanket,
  Seventeen times as high as the moon;
And where she was going I couldn't but ask it,
  For in her hand she carried a broom.

Old woman, old woman, old woman, quoth I,
  O whither, O whither, O whither, so high?
To brush the cobwebs off the sky!
  Shall I go with thee? Yes, by-and-by.

## THERE WAS AN OLD WOMAN

There was an old woman who lived in a shoe,
She had so many children she didn't know what to do;
She gave them some broth without any bread;
She whipped them all soundly and put them to bed.

## A WEE BIT WIFIE

There was a wee bit wifie,
  Who lived in a shoe;
She had so many bairns,
  She kenn'd not what to do.
She gaed to the market
  To buy a sheep-head;
When she came back
  They were a' lying dead.
She went to the wright,
  To get them a coffin;
When she came back,
  They were a' lying laughing.
She gaed up the stair,
  To ring the bell;
The bell rope broke,
  And down she fell.

## BOYS AND GIRLS

Boys and girls come out to play,
The moon doth shine as bright as day;
Leave your supper and leave your sleep,
And join your playfellows in the street;
Come with a whoop and come with a call,
Come with a good will or not at all;
Up the ladder and down the wall,
A halfpenny loaf will serve us all;
You find milk, and I'll find flour,
And we'll have a pudding in half an hour.

## HERE WE GO LOOBY-LOO

Here we go Looby-loo
Here we go Looby-light
Here we go Looby-loo
All on a Saturday night.

## SALLY

Sally go round the sun,
Sally go round the moon,
Sally go round the chimney-pots
On a Saturday afternoon.

## RING-A-RING O' ROSES

Ring-a-ring o' roses,
A pocket full of posies,
  A-tishoo! A-tishoo!
We all fall down.

The cows are in the meadow,
Lying fast asleep,
  A-tishoo! A-tishoo!
We all get up again.

## BLIND MAN'S BUFF

Blind man, blind man,
  Sure you can't see?
Turn round three times,
  And try to catch me.
Turn east, turn west,
  Catch as you can,
Did you think you'd caught me?
  Blind, blind man!

## HINX, MINX

Hinx, minx, the old witch winks,
The fat begins to fry,
Nobody at home but Jumping Joan,
Father, Mother and I.
Stick, stock, stone dead,
Blind man can't see,
Every knave will have a slave,
You or I must be he.

## ICKLE OCKLE

Ickle ockle, blue bockle,
  Fishes in the sea,
If you want a pretty maid,
  Please choose me.

## PAT-A-CAKE

Pat-a-cake, pat-a-cake, baker's man,
  Bake me a cake as fast as you can;
Pat it and prick it, and mark it with T.
Put it in the oven for Tommy and me.

# HERE WE GO ROUND THE MULBERRY BUSH

Here we go round the mulberry bush,
  The mulberry bush, the mulberry bush,
Here we go round the mulberry bush,
  On a cold and frosty morning.

This is the way we wash our clothes,
  Wash our clothes, wash our clothes,
This is the way we wash our clothes,
  On a cold and frosty morning.

This is the way we iron our clothes,
  Iron our clothes, iron our clothes,
This is the way we iron our clothes,
  On a cold and frosty morning.

This is the way we sweep our rooms,
  Sweep our rooms, sweep our rooms,
This is the way we sweep our rooms,
  On a cold and frosty morning.

94

This is the way we mend our shoes,
  Mend our shoes, mend our shoes,
This is the way we mend our shoes,
  On a cold and frosty morning.

This is the way we wash our hands,
  Wash our hands, wash our hands,
This is the way we wash our hands,
  On a cold and frosty morning.

This is the way we do our hair,
  Do our hair, do our hair,
This is the way we do our hair,
  On a cold and frosty morning.

This is the way we go to school,
  Go to school, go to school,
This is the way we go to school,
  On a cold and frosty morning.

This is the way we come back from school,
  Come back from school, come back from school,
This is the way we come back from school,
  On a cold and frosty morning.

95

## COCK A DOODLE DOO!

Cock a doodle doo!
My dame has lost her shoe,
My master's lost his fiddling stick,
And knows not what to do.

Cock a doodle doo!
What is my dame to do?
Till master finds his fiddling stick,
She'll dance without her shoe.

Cock a doodle doo!
My dame has found her shoe,
And master's found his fiddling stick,
Sing doodle doodle doo.

Cock a doodle doo!
My dame will dance with you,
While master fiddles his fiddling stick
For dame and doodle doo.

## FIDDLE-DE-DEE

Fiddle-de-dee, fiddle-de-dee,
The fly shall marry the humble-bee.
They went to the church, and married was she:
The fly has married the humble-bee.

## LADYBIRD, LADYBIRD

Ladybird, ladybird,
  Fly away home,
Your house is on fire
  And your children all gone;
All except one
  And that's little Ann
And she has crept under
  The frying pan.

## PIGGYBACK

Matthew, Mark, Luke and John,
Hold my horse till I leap on,
Hold him steady, hold him sure,
And I'll get over the misty moor.

## I LOST MY MARE

I lost my mare in Lincoln Lane,
I'll never find her there again;
  She lost a shoe,
    And then lost two,
And threw her rider in the drain.

## I HAD A LITTLE PONY

I had a little pony,
  His name was Dapple Gray;
I lent him to a lady
  To ride a mile away.
She whipped him, she lashed him,
  She rode him through the mire;
I would not lend my pony now,
  For all the lady's hire.

## GIDDY UP

Giddy up horsey,
Don't say stop,
Just let your feet
Go clippety clop,
Clippety clop and hippity hop;
Giddy up,
We're homeward bound.

## YANKEE DOODLE

Yankee Doodle came to town,
   Riding on a pony.
He stuck a feather in his cap
   And called it macaroni.

## SEE-SAW, SACRADOWN

See-saw, sacradown,
Which is the way to London town?
One foot up and the other foot down,
That is the way to London town.

## LONDON BRIDGE

London Bridge is broken down,
Broken down, broken down,
London Bridge is broken down,
My fair lady.

Build it up with wood and clay,
Wood and clay, wood and clay,
Build it up with wood and clay,
My fair lady.

Wood and clay will wash away,
Wash away, wash away,
Wood and clay will wash away,
My fair lady.

Build it up with bricks and mortar,
Bricks and mortar, bricks and mortar,
Build it up with bricks and mortar,
My fair lady.

Bricks and mortar will not stay,
Will not stay, will not stay,
Bricks and mortar will not stay,
My fair lady.

Build it up with iron and steel,
Iron and steel, iron and steel,
Build it up with iron and steel,
My fair lady.

Iron and steel will bend and bow,
Bend and bow, bend and bow,
Iron and steel will bend and bow,
My fair lady.

Build it up with silver and gold,
Silver and gold, silver and gold,
Build it up with silver and gold,
My fair lady.

Silver and gold will be stolen away,
Stolen away, stolen away,
Silver and gold will be stolen away,
My fair lady.

Set a man to watch all night,
Watch all night, watch all night,
Set a man to watch all night,
My fair lady.

Suppose the man should fall asleep,
Fall asleep, fall asleep,
Suppose the man should fall asleep,
My fair lady.

Give him a pipe to smoke all night,
Smoke all night, smoke all night,
Give him a pipe to smoke all night,
My fair lady.

## ORANGES AND LEMONS

Bull's-eyes and targets,
Say the bells of St Marg'ret's.

Brickbats and tiles,
Say the bells of St Giles'.

Oranges and lemons,
Say the bells of St Clement's.

Pancakes and fritters,
Say the bells of St Peter's.

Two sticks and an apple,
Say the bells at Whitechapel.

Old Father Baldpate,
Say the slow bells at Aldgate.

Maids in white aprons,
Say the bells at St Catherine's.

Pokers and tongs,
Say the bells at St John's.

Kettles and pans,
Say the bells at St Anne's.

You owe me five farthings,
Say the bells of St Martin's.

When will you pay me?
Say the bells at Old Bailey.

When I grow rich,
Say the bells at Shoreditch.

Pray, when will that be?
Say the bells at Stepney.

I'm sure I don't know,
Says the great bell at Bow.

Here comes a candle to light you to bed,
Here comes a chopper to chop off your head!

## THE MERCHANTS OF LONDON

Hey diddle dinkety, poppety, pet,
The merchants of London they wear scarlet,
Silk in the collar and gold in the hem,
So merrily march the merchant men.

## POP GOES THE WEASEL!

Up and down the City Road,
  In and out the Eagle,
That's the way the money goes,
  Pop goes the weasel!

Half a pound of tuppenny rice,
  Half a pound of treacle,
Mix it up and make it nice,
  Pop goes the weasel!

Every night when I go out
  The monkey's on the table;
Take a stick and knock it off,
  Pop goes the weasel!

## GREGORY GRIGGS

Gregory Griggs, Gregory Griggs,
Had twenty-seven different wigs.
He wore them up, he wore them down,
To please the people of the town;
He wore them east, he wore them west,
But he never could tell which he loved the best.

## GOOSEY GANDER

Goosey, goosey, gander,
Whither shall I wander?
Upstairs and downstairs
And in my lady's chamber.
There I met an old man
Who would not say his prayers,
I took him by the left leg
And threw him down the stairs.

105

## SUGAR AND SPICE

What are little boys made of?
What are little boys made of?
  Frogs and snails
  And puppy-dogs' tails,
That's what little boys are made of.

What are little girls made of?
What are little girls made of?
  Sugar and spice
  And all things nice,
That's what little girls are made of.

## MONDAY'S CHILD

Monday's child is fair of face,
Tuesday's child is full of grace,
Wednesday's child is full of woe,
Thursday's child has far to go,
Friday's child is loving and giving,
Saturday's child works hard for a living,
And the child that is born on the Sabbath day
Is bonny and wise and good and gay.

## THERE WAS A LITTLE GIRL

There was a little girl,
  Who had a little curl,
Right in the middle of her forehead;
  And when she was good,
  She was very very good,
And when she was bad she was horrid.

She stood on her head,
  On her little truckle bed,
With nobody by for to hinder;
  She screamed and she squalled,
  She yelled and she bawled,
And drummed her little heels against the winder.

## SULKY SUE

Here's Sulky Sue:
What shall we do?
Turn her face to the wall
Till she comes to.

## JUMPING JOAN

Here am I,
Little Jumping Joan;
When nobody's with me
I'm all alone.

## LITTLE TOMMY TUCKER

Little Tommy Tucker
Sings for his supper;
What shall we give him?
White bread and butter.

How shall he cut it
Without e'er a knife?
How shall he marry
Without e'er a wife?

## CROSS PATCH

Cross Patch lift the latch
Sit by the fire and spin;
Take a cup and drink it up,
Then call your neighbours in.

## The Pasty

Deedle deedle dumpling, my son John,
Ate a pasty five feet long;
He bit it once, he bit it twice,
Oh, my goodness, it was full of mice!

## Diddle, Diddle, Dumpling

Diddle, diddle, dumpling, my son John,
Went to bed with his trousers on;
One shoe off, and one shoe on,
Diddle, diddle, dumpling, my son John.

## ROBIN THE BOBBIN

Robin the Bobbin, the big-bellied Ben,
He ate more meat than fourscore men;
He ate a cow, he ate a calf,
He ate a butcher and a half,
He ate a church, he ate a steeple,
He ate the priest and all the people!
A cow and a calf,
An ox and a half,
A church and a steeple,
And all the good people,
And yet he complained that his
   stomach wasn't full.

## RUMPTY-IDDITY

Rumpty-iddity, row, row, row,
If I had a good supper,
   I could eat it now.

## OLD BONIFACE

Old Boniface he loved good cheer,
　And took his glass of Burton,
And when the nights grew sultry hot
　He slept without a shirt on.

## MRS MASON

Mrs Mason bought a basin,
Mrs Tyson said, What a nice 'un,
What did it cost? said Mrs Frost,
Half a crown, said Mrs Brown,
Did it indeed, said Mrs Reed,
It did for certain, said Mrs Burton,
Then Mrs Nix up to her tricks
Threw the basin on the bricks.

## JACK HORNER

Little Jack Horner
Sat in a corner,
Eating a Christmas pie;
He put in his thumb,
And pulled out a plum,
And said, What a good boy am I!

## LITTLE JACK HORNER?

Little Jack Horner
Sat in a corner,
Eating his curds and whey;
There came a big spider,
Who sat down beside her,
And the dish ran away with the spoon.

*"Daddy, you haven't got it right!"*

## CAKES AND CUSTARD

When Jacky's a good boy,
He shall have cakes and custard;
But when he does nothing but cry,
He shall have nothing but mustard.

## WORK AND PLAY

All work and no play
Makes Jack a dull boy;
All play and no work
Makes Jack a mere toy.

## JACK SPRAT

Jack Sprat could eat no fat,
　His wife could eat no lean;
And so between the two of them,
　They licked the platter clean.

## POLLY PUT THE KETTLE ON

Polly put the kettle on,
Polly put the kettle on,
Polly put the kettle on,
  We'll all have tea.

Sukey take it off again,
Sukey take it off again,
Sukey take it off again,
  They've all gone away.

## PEASE-PUDDING

Pease-pudding hot,
Pease-pudding cold,
Pease-pudding in the pot,
  Nine days old.
Some like it hot,
Some like it cold,
Some like it in the pot,
  Nine days old.

## DAVY DUMPLING

Davy Davy Dumpling,
Boil him in the pot;
Sugar him and butter him,
And eat him while he's hot.

## HOT CROSS BUNS!

Hot cross buns! Hot cross buns!
One a penny, two a penny,
Hot cross buns!
If your daughters do not like them
Give them to your sons;
But if you haven't any of these pretty little elves,
You cannot do better than eat them yourselves.

## JACK-A-DANDY

Nauty Pauty Jack-a-Dandy
Stole a piece of sugar candy
From the grocer's shoppy-shop,
And away did hoppy-hop.

## THE HOUSE THAT JACK BUILT

This is the house that Jack built.

This is the malt that lay in the house that Jack built.

This is the rat that ate the malt
that lay in the house that Jack built.

This is the cat that killed the rat that ate the malt
that lay in the house that Jack built.

This is the dog that worried the cat that killed the rat
that ate the malt that lay in the house that Jack built.

This is the cow with the crumpled horn that tossed the dog
that worried the cat that killed the rat
that ate the malt that lay in the house that Jack built.

This is the maiden all forlorn that milked the cow with the
crumpled horn that tossed the dog that worried the cat that
killed the rat that ate the malt that lay in the house that Jack built.

This is the man all tattered and torn that kissed the maiden all
forlorn that milked the cow that tossed the dog that worried the
cat that killed the rat that ate the malt that lay in the house that Jack built.

This is the priest all shaven and shorn that married the man all tattered and torn that kissed the maiden all forlorn that milked the cow that tossed the dog that worried the cat that killed the rat that ate the malt that lay in the house that Jack built.

This is the cock that crowed in the morn that waked the priest all shaven and shorn that married the man all tattered and torn that kissed the maiden all forlorn that milked the cow that tossed the dog that worried the cat that killed the rat that ate the malt that lay in the house that Jack built.

This is the farmer sowing his corn that kept the cock that crowed in the morn that waked the priest all shaven and shorn that married the man all tattered and torn that kissed the maiden all forlorn that milked the cow that tossed the dog that worried the cat that killed the rat that ate the malt that lay in the house that Jack built.

## OLD MOTHER HUBBARD

Old Mother Hubbard
Went to the cupboard,
To fetch her poor dog a bone;
But when she got there
The cupboard was bare
And so the poor dog had none.

She went to the baker's
To buy him some bread;
But when she came back
The poor dog was dead.

She went to the undertaker's
To buy him a coffin;
But when she came back
The poor dog was laughing.

She took a clean dish
To get him some tripe;
But when she came back
He was smoking a pipe.

She went to the tavern
For white wine and red;
But when she came back
The dog stood on his head.

She went to the fruiterer's
To buy him some fruit;
But when she came back
He was playing the flute.

She went to the tailor's
  To buy him a coat;
But when she came back
  He was riding a goat.

She went to the barber's
  To buy him a wig;
But when she came back
  He was dancing a jig.

She went to the hatter's
  To buy him a hat;
But when she came back
  He was feeding the cat.

She went to the cobbler's
  To buy him some shoes;
But when she came back
  He was reading the news.

She went to the hosier's
  To buy him some hose;
But when she came back
  He was dressed in his clothes.

The dame made a curtsey,
  The dog made a bow;
The dame said, Your servant,
  The dog said, Bow-wow.

## OLD MOTHER GOOSE

Old Mother Goose,
　When she wanted to wander,
Would ride through the air
　On a very fine gander.

Mother Goose had a house,
　'Twas built in a wood,
Where an owl at the door
　For sentinel stood.

She had a son Jack,
　A plain-looking lad,
He was not very good,
　Nor yet very bad.

She sent him to market,
　A live goose he bought;
See, mother, says he,
　I have not been for nought.

Jack's goose and her gander
　Grew very fond;
They'd both eat together,
　Or swim in the pond.

Jack found one fine morning,
　As I have been told,
His goose had laid him
　An egg of pure gold.

Jack ran to his mother
　The news for to tell,
She called him a good boy,
　And said it was well.

Jack sold his gold egg
　To a merchant untrue,
Who cheated him out of
　A half of his due.

Then Jack went a-courting
　A lady so gay,
As fair as the lily,
　And sweet as the May.

The merchant and squire
　Soon came at his back,
And began to belabour
　The sides of poor Jack.

Then old Mother Goose
　That instant came in,
And turned her son Jack
　Into famed Harlequin.

She then with her wand
　Touched the lady so fine,
And turned her at once
　Into sweet Columbine.

The gold egg in the sea
  Was thrown away then,
When an odd fish brought her
  The egg back again.


The merchant then vowed
  The goose he would kill,
Resolving at once
  His pockets to fill.

Jack's mother came in,
  And caught the goose soon,
And mounting its back,
  Flew up to the moon.

Higher than a house,
Higher than a tree;
Oh, whatever can that be?

In spring I look gay,
Decked in comely array,
In summer more clothing I wear;
When colder it grows,
I fling off my clothes,
And in winter quite naked appear.

If all the world were paper,
And all the sea were ink,
If all the trees were bread and cheese,
What should we have to drink?

*It's enough to make a man like me
Scratch his head and think.*

I'm called by the name of a man,
Yet am as little as a mouse;
When winter comes I love to be
With my red target near the house.

Two brothers we are,
Great burdens we bear,
All day we are bitterly pressed,
Yet this I must say–
We are full all the day,
And empty when we go to rest.

Purple, yellow, red and green,
The king cannot reach it, nor yet the queen;
Nor can Old Noll, whose power is great,
Tell me this riddle while I count eight.

Two legs sat upon three legs
With one leg in his lap;
In comes four legs
And runs away with one leg;
Up jumps two legs,
Catches up three legs,
Throws it after four legs,
And makes him bring back one leg.

Round and round the rugged rock
The ragged rascal ran,
How many Rs are there in *that*?
Now tell me if you can.

Betty Botter bought some butter,
But, she said, the butter's bitter;
If I put it in my batter
It will make my batter bitter,
But a bit of better butter
Will make my batter better.
So she bought a bit of butter
Better than her bitter butter,
And she put it in her batter
And the batter was not bitter.
So 'twas better Betty Botter
Bought a bit of better butter.

Billy Button bought a butter'd biscuit;
Did Billy Button buy a butter'd biscuit?
If Billy Button bought a butter'd biscuit,
Where's the butter'd biscuit Billy Button bought?

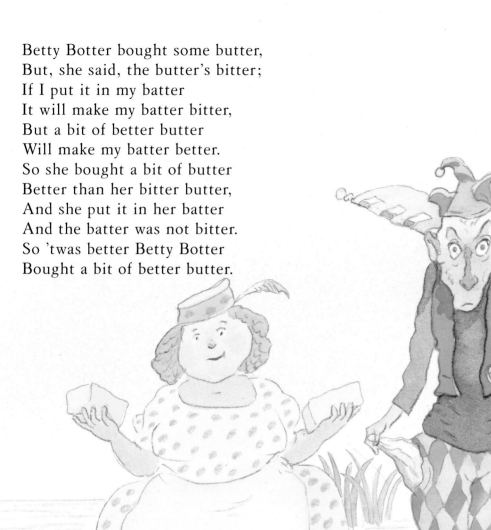

Moses supposes his toeses are roses,
But Moses supposes erroneously;
For nobody's toeses are posies of roses
As Moses supposes his toeses to be.

Peter Piper picked a peck of pickled pepper;
A peck of pickled pepper Peter Piper picked.
If Peter Piper picked a peck of pickled pepper,
Where's the peck of pickled pepper Peter Piper picked?

Davy Dolldrum dream'd he drove a dragon;
Did Davy Dolldrum dream he drove a dragon?
If Davy Dolldrum dream'd he drove a dragon,
Where's the dragon Davy Dolldrum dream'd he drove?

How much wood would a woodchuck chuck
If a woodchuck could chuck wood?
He would chuck as much wood as a woodchuck
  could chuck.
If a woodchuck could chuck wood.

Swan swam over the sea,
  Swim, swan, swim!
Swan swam back again,
  Well swum, swan!

127

## COBBLER, COBBLER

Cobbler, cobbler, mend my shoe,
Get it done by half past two;
Stitch it up, and stitch it down,
Then I'll give you half a crown.

## RUB-A-DUB-DUB

Rub-a-dub-dub,
Three men in a tub,
And how do you think they got there?
The butcher, the baker,
The candlestick-maker,
They all jumped out of a rotten potato,
'Twas enough to make a man stare.

## BARBER, BARBER

Barber, barber, shave a pig,
How many hairs to make a wig?
Four-and-twenty, that's enough,
Give the barber a pinch of snuff.

## CHARLEY, CHARLEY

Charley, Charley,
Stole the barley
Out of the baker's shop.
The baker came out
And gave him a clout,
Which made poor Charley hop.

## MY MAMMY'S MAID

Dingty diddlety, my mammy's maid,
  She stole some oranges, I'm afraid;
Some in her pocket, some in her sleeve,
  She stole oranges, I do believe!

## DICKERY, DICKERY, DARE

Dickery, dickery, dare,
The pig flew up in the air;
The man in brown
Soon brought him down,
Dickery, dickery, dare.

## FISHES SWIM

Fishes swim in water clear,
Birds fly up into the air;
Serpents creep along the ground,
Boys and girls run round and round.

## JERRY HALL

Jerry Hall
He is so small,
A rat could eat him,
Hat and all.

## TOMMY TITTLEMOUSE

Little Tommy Tittlemouse
Lived in a little house;
He caught fishes
In other men's ditches.

## THREE YOUNG RATS

Three young rats with black felt hats,
Three young ducks with white straw flats,
Three young dogs with curling tails,
Three young cats with demi-veils,
Went out to walk with two young pigs
In satin vests and sorrel wigs.
But suddenly it chanced to rain
And so they all went home again.

## HODDLEY, PODDLEY

Hoddley, poddley, puddles and fogs,
Cats are to marry the poodle dogs;
Cats in blue jackets and dogs in red hats,
What will become of the mice and the rats?

### A Frog He Would A-wooing Go

A frog he would a-wooing go,
  Heigh ho! says Rowley,
A frog he would a-wooing go,
Whether his mother would let him or no.
  With a rowley, powley, gammon and spinach,
  Heigh ho! says Anthony Rowley.

So off he set with his opera hat,
  Heigh ho! says Rowley,
So off he set with his opera hat,
And on the road he met with a rat,
  With a rowley, powley, gammon and spinach,
  Heigh ho! says Anthony Rowley.

Pray, Mr Rat, will you go with me?
  Heigh ho! says Rowley,
Pray, Mr Rat, will you go with me,
Kind Mrs Mousey for to see?
  With a rowley, powley, gammon and spinach,
  Heigh ho! says Anthony Rowley.

They came to the door of Mousey's hall,
  Heigh ho! says Rowley,
They gave a loud knock, and they gave a loud call.
  With a rowley, powley, gammon and spinach,
  Heigh ho! says Anthony Rowley.

Pray, Mrs Mouse, are you within?
  Heigh ho! says Rowley,
Oh yes, kind sirs, I'm sitting to spin.
  With a rowley, powley, gammon and spinach,
  Heigh ho! says Anthony Rowley.

Pray, Mrs Mouse, will you give us some beer?
  Heigh ho! says Rowley,
For Froggy and I are fond of good cheer.
  With a rowley, powley, gammon and spinach,
  Heigh ho! says Anthony Rowley.

Pray, Mr Frog, will you give us a song?
　　Heigh ho! says Rowley,
Let it be something that's not very long.
　　With a rowley, powley, gammon and spinach,
　　Heigh ho! says Anthony Rowley.

Indeed, Mrs Mouse, replied Mr Frog,
　　Heigh ho! says Rowley,
A cold has made me as hoarse as a dog.
　　With a rowley, powley, gammon and spinach,
　　Heigh ho! says Anthony Rowley.

Since you have a cold, Mr Frog, Mousey said,
　　Heigh ho! says Rowley,
I'll sing you a song that I have just made.
　　With a rowley, powley, gammon and spinach,
　　Heigh ho! says Anthony Rowley.

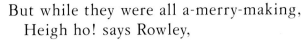

But while they were all a-merry-making,
　　Heigh ho! says Rowley,
A cat and her kittens came tumbling in.
　　With a rowley, powley, gammon and spinach,
　　Heigh ho! says Anthony Rowley.

The cat she seized the rat by the crown,
　　Heigh ho! says Rowley,
The kittens they pulled the little mouse down.
　　With a rowley, powley, gammon and spinach,
　　Heigh ho! says Anthony Rowley.

This put Mr Frog in a terrible fright,
  Heigh ho! says Rowley,
He took up his hat and he wished them good-night.
  With a rowley, powley, gammon and spinach,
  Heigh ho! says Anthony Rowley.

But as Froggy was crossing over a brook,
  Heigh ho! says Rowley,
A lily-white duck came and gobbled him up.
  With a rowley, powley, gammon and spinach,
  Heigh ho! says Anthony Rowley.

So there was an end of one, two, three,
  Heigh ho! says Rowley,
The rat, the mouse, and the frog-ee.
  With a rowley, powley, gammon and spinach,
  Heigh ho! says Anthony Rowley.

# TWEEDLEDUM AND TWEEDLEDEE

Tweedledum and Tweedledee,
  Agreed to fight a battle,
For Tweedledum said Tweedledee
  Had spoiled his nice new rattle.
Just then flew by a monstrous crow
  As black as a tar barrel,
Which frightened both the heroes so,
  They quite forgot their quarrel.

# THE LION AND THE UNICORN

The lion and the unicorn
  Were fighting for the crown;
The lion beat the unicorn
  All around the town.

Some gave them white bread,
  And some gave them brown;
Some gave them plum cake
  And drummed them out of town.

### SEE A PIN

See a pin and pick it up
And all the day you'll have good luck.
See a pin and let it lie
Wish you'll not have cause to cry.

### EARLY TO BED

Early to bed, and early to rise,
Makes a man healthy, wealthy and wise.

### DOCTOR FOSTER

Doctor Foster is a good man,
He teaches children all he can;
Reading, writing, arithmetic,
And doesn't forget to use his stick;
When he does he makes them dance
Out of England into France,
Out of France into Spain,
Round the world and back again.

## DOCTOR FOSTER

Doctor Foster went to Gloucester
In a shower of rain;
He stepped in a puddle,
Right up to his middle,
And never went there again.

## ONE MISTY, MOISTY MORNING

One misty, moisty morning,
When cloudy was the weather,
There I met an old man
Clothed all in leather;
Clothed all in leather,
With cap under his chin.
How do you do, and how do you do,
And how do you do again!

Rain, rain, go away,
Come again another day,
Little Johnny wants to play.

Rain, rain, go to Spain,
Never show your face again.

Rain before seven,
Fine before eleven.

Rain on the green grass,
And rain on the tree,
Rain on the house-top,
But not on me.

A sunshiny shower
Won't last half an hour.

## INCEY WINCEY SPIDER

Incey wincey spider
Climbed the water spout,
Down came the rain
And washed poor Incey out.
Out came the sun
And dried up all the rain,
So Incey wincey spider
Climbed the spout again.

## IT'S RAINING, IT'S POURING

It's raining, it's pouring,
The old man is snoring.
He got into bed
And bumped his head
And couldn't get up in the morning.

## THE SKY

Red sky at night,
Shepherd's delight;
Red sky in the morning,
Shepherd's warning.

141

## THERE WAS A CROOKED MAN

There was a crooked man,
  And he walked a crooked mile,
He found a crooked sixpence
  Against a crooked stile;
He bought a crooked cat,
  Which caught a crooked mouse,
And they all lived together
  In a little crooked house.

## THE MAN IN THE WILDERNESS

The man in the wilderness asked me
　How many strawberries grew in the sea?
I answered him, as I thought good,
　As many as red herrings grew in the wood.

## TELL TALE

Tell tale, nit!
Your tongue shall be slit,
And all the dogs in the town
Shall have a little bit.

143

## MY MOTHER SAID

My mother said
That I never should
Play with the gypsies
In the wood;
If I did she would say,
Naughty girl to disobey.
Your hair shan't curl,
Your shoes shan't shine,
You naughty girl,
You shan't be mine.
My father said
That if I did
He'd bang my head
With the teapot lid.

The wood was dark
The grass was green,
Up comes Sally
With a tambourine,
Alpaca frock,
New scarf-shawl,
White straw bonnet
And a pink parasol.
I went to the river —
No ship to get across,
I paid ten shillings
For an old blind horse;
I up on his back
And off in a crack,
Sally tell my mother
I shall never come back.

145

## THE KEY OF THE KINGDOM

This is the key of the kingdom:
In that kingdom there is a city,
In that city there is a town,
In that town there is a street,
In that street there is a lane,
In that lane there is a yard,
In that yard there is a house,
In that house there is a room,
In that room there is a bed,
In that bed there is a basket,
 In that basket there are some flowers.

Flowers in the basket,
Basket on the bed,
Bed in the room,
Room in the house,
House in the yard,
Yard in the lane,
Lane in the street,
Street in the town,
Town in the city,
City in the kingdom:
  And this is the key of the kingdom.

## THE MAN IN THE MOON

The man in the moon
Came tumbling down,
And asked his way to Norwich.
He went by the south,
And burnt his mouth
With supping hot pease-porridge.

## BEDTIME

Come, let's to bed,
Says Sleepyhead;
Tarry a while, says Slow;
Put on the pot,
Says Greedygut,
We'll sup before we go.

## BEDTIME

Down with the lambs
Up with the lark,
Run to bed children
Before it gets dark.

## BABYLON

How many miles to Babylon?
Threescore miles and ten.
Can I get there by candlelight?
Yes, and back again.
If your heels are nimble and light,
You can get there by candlelight.

## UP TO BED

Up the wooden hill
  To Bedfordshire,
Down Sheet Lane
  To Blanket Fair.

## BED

Go to bed first,
A golden purse;
Go to bed second,
A golden pheasant;
Go to bed third,
A golden bird.

149

### STAR LIGHT

Star light, star bright,
First star I see tonight,
I wish I may, I wish I might,
Have the wish I wish tonight.

### MATTHEW, MARK, LUKE AND JOHN

Matthew, Mark, Luke and John,
Bless the bed that I lie on.
    Four corners to my bed,
    Four angels round my head;
    One to watch and one to pray
    And two to bear my soul away.

### THE MOON

The moon shines bright,
The stars give light,
And little Nanny Button-cap
Will come tomorrow night.

### GOING TO BED

Go to bed late,
Stay very small;
Go to bed early,
Grow very tall.

### A PRAYER

Now I lay me down to sleep,
I pray the Lord my soul to keep;
And if I die before I wake,
I pray the Lord my soul to take.

### GOD BLESS ME

I see the moon,
  And the moon sees me;
God bless the moon,
  And God bless me.

# INDEX OF FIRST LINES

In selecting the rhymes for this book, many sources were consulted.
Of the published material, the most inspirational were:

James Orchard Halliwell's
*Popular Rhymes and Nursery Tales*
(Frederick Warne and Co., 1849) and
*The Nursery Rhymes and Nursery Tales of England*
(Frederick Warne and Co., fifth edition, c. 1860);
*The Baby's Bouquet*
arranged and decorated by Walter Crane
(Frederick Warne and Co., 1879);
*Mother Goose*
illustrated by Kate Greenaway
(George Routledge and Sons, 1881);
W. F. Prideaux's *Mother Goose's Melody*
(A. H. Bullen, 1904);
Iona and Peter Opie's
*The Oxford Dictionary of Nursery Rhymes*
(OUP, 1973 edition) and
*The Oxford Nursery Rhyme Book*
(OUP, 1984 edition);
William S. and Ceil Baring-Gould's
*The Annotated Mother Goose*
(New American Library edition, 1976);
and *The Nursery Rhyme Book*
edited by Andrew Lang
(Omega Books, 1985).

Rhymes selected from the Opies' *Oxford Dictionary of Nursery Rhymes*
and *Oxford Nursery Rhyme Book* are reprinted
by permission of Oxford University Press.